Diaspora
Hallucinations

Dr Hashem Alhussein &
Dr Thaier Alhusain

To our wounded land. To our beloved -Ar-Raqqah. To all the displaced, the refugees and the heroes who help them. To my mother and father's blessed souls. To my wife and children, I dedicate this book.

Dr Hashem Alhussein

Contents

Our Neighbour
is Beautiful

جَارَتُنا جَمِيلَةٌ

Our neighbour's beauty is a wonder to behold,
Her cheek soft and gentle, her smile so bold.
Her small lips are made for a tender kiss,
Her eyes shine bright, her eyes I miss.

Her morning begins with a gentle glow,
Her waist a secret kept below.
Her lips sweet as sugar, her hair a braid
A red rose adorns it, a gentle shade.

She walks with grace, like a deer in the woods,
Her humility easy, her kindness for good.
Her beauty shines through, both confident and shy,
Like a smile on roses, that fill the sky.

With the scent of perfume and basil so strong
Her lips, soft and luscious, whisper a sweet song.
Our neighbour is beautiful, a sight to see
 A ray of sunshine, a gift to me.

H.A.

The Third Body

الْجسدُ الثَّالِثُ

Two hearts, both made a vow, to give a gift to the gods,
She, from the city, he, from the village, their love against the
    odds.
Her eyes ask, "Where did this boy come from?" young and fresh,
    she inquires,
Her breasts, yet to blossom, pushing under silken attire.

And he, "Where did this girl come from?" with clouds in his
    eyes,
His body, formed and mature, but still thirsts, no rain in sight.
She reads, in city slang, poetry that electrifies,
And he, a villager boy, is touched, yet, no rain flies.

"What does it mean to be a villager?" she asked, he replies,
"A man like your father, skin dark, hands big, who tames the
    land and skies."
"Do you know how to kiss?" she asked, his heart burst in a dash,
"Villagers have no time for love, surviving day's crash."

But she pulls him close, to teach, the art of a city kiss,
Their lips meet, and at last, the clouds of love, they unleash.

H.A.

An Ode to the Playful Girl

الفَتَاة اللَّعُوب

Her waist like a dewy branch, so gracefully bent,
Sprints like a gazelle, aggressively spent,
Like golden sparks flying from a stove's fire,
Her every movement, a testament to her desire.

A prisoner of passion, tied to the gift of love,
Her beauty so great, my senses were not enough,
Two moles on her cheek, like grains of prostration,
The muezzin lost in her light, called the dawn prayer without a

    station.

The imam prayed without direction, the mosque without a crowd,
Ignoring my people, she whispered, "I'm yours, you should be
    proud."
She offered me wine, and her lips, so sweet,
Her chest sighed, and I pressed against her, as if to complete.

But when my movements increased, she threw me away,
Saying, "Stop crossing your limits, do not transgress,
You'll have me soon, after spring has come,
You're a cosset now, when you're a ram, do come."

H.A.

The Siege of
the Snail

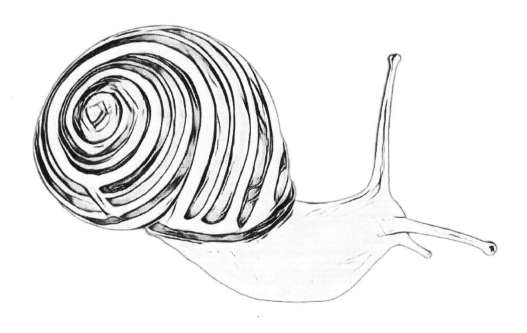

حِصَارُ
القَوقَعة

A smile so forced, so sad it seems,
Adam wears it even in his dreams.
Different born, some mock his ways,
Their laughter ringing through the days.

Innocent and kind, a soul so pure,
He gives his all, and always more.
Most days he stays within his home,
Drawing kingdoms where the sun has shone.

A snail, once caught, became a joke,
The teenager pointed, "Look, it's broke!"
The kids they laughed, but Adam saw,
The snail trapped in a salt circle's claw.

Its eyes, once wide, now shrinking down,
Tears left behind in a single frown.
But still, it crept, and tried anew,
Its eyes still dribbling morning dew.

"Please stay inside," Adam whispered low,
"No one can hurt you, don't you know?"
His father called, but still he stayed,
Gazing at the snail, he wouldn't be swayed.

"They're hurting Adam, Papa," he said,
"You must help, or it will be dead."
Adam stood firm, his eyes fixed on,
The snail's journey, until it was gone.

T.A.

Different Recipe, Similar Taste

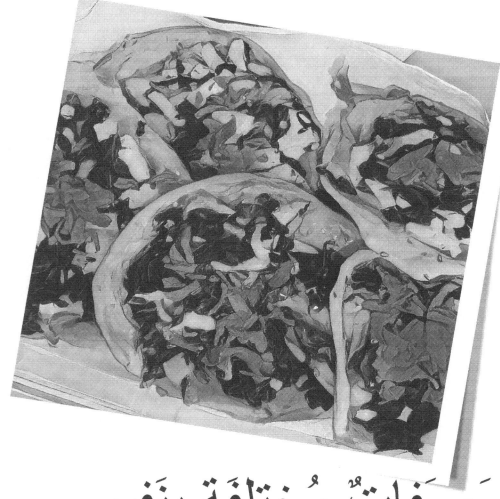

وَصَفاتٌ مُختلِفَة بنَفس الطَّعم

A neat little notebook, organized with care,
Mum's treasure trove of recipes, so rare.
The ink was scented, red and blue,
And every time it was opened, a fragrance flew.

Each title was adorned with little blue stars,
And a sketch of the finished dish at the bottom left bars
Was it love or competition that fuelled her fire?
The question I often pondered, was it need, or desire.

Aunt Nadia, selfish with her recipes untold,
Refused to share, Mum's reverse engineering bold.
"Why can't she share, like me," she'd always say,
And I'd think, "Because you're too kind, it's not okay."

But as we grew older, we came to understand,
That recipes are just recipes, not a command.
It's not the recipe that makes a meal divine,
It's the person who cooks it, the house, and the time.
The people who share it, the memories made,
That's what makes a meal truly great.

T.A.

The Bard of the Wood

شاعر الغَابة

Amidst the grand garden's vista fair,
A daughter stood with grace beyond compare,
Her hair of green, a shining hue,
As raindrops twirl in morning dew.

She spoke to me, the bard of the wood,
Of loss, of melodies that were once good.
O Poet of the forest's wild domain,
Your words evoke emotions, so pained.

Every bloom recalls your name,
Your roots, once nourished, now proclaim.
Your rough bark holds images, so bold,
Of love and hate, a story untold.

H.A.

Him and Her

هو و هِي

Her:
I speak of vows broken and faith lost
Of promises made but never fulfilled.
My eyes are tired of waiting, my heart weary
I ask, My Love, where did it all end?
Your slurred words once bound me,
But now, a thousand tomorrows have passed
And still you haven't kept your word.
But I pray for forgiveness, for I still love you.

Him:
Congratulations on a happy union.
May his wallet warm you, his words please,
But what of the one who waits for you?
The one who still holds onto your promises.
I left in search of a pearl I had promised,
And now you rest in an erased grave,
In your heart, I will always be the traveller
Who promised to visit, to bring you a precious gift.

Tomorrow your groom will come with his wealth
But what good is money, when the heart is lost?
He laments the end of the year,
Where will the dowry go from here?
What colours will he find in your eyes?

Poverty, My Love, is a science I'd learned too well.
You taught me oppression and sad love Illusions and heartbreak,
all in the name of poverty.
It's impossible to think, to see past the lustre
And poverty still haunts us, a part of our history.

Broken promises, disappointments in love
These are the stories that mark us, that shape us.
But still, I'll hold onto hope, onto love,
For it's these very things that keep me alive.

H.A.

An Ode to a Piece of Heaven

قِطعة مِن

الجَنَّة

A tree, with a scent divine,
I sat, entranced, beneath its vine.
"How can I cut a piece of heaven down?"
The architect's advice, I'd wearily frown.

So, a house I built around the tree,
With a gap in the roof for all to see.
Transparent plastic, for winter's chill
Thick cardboard, in summer's scorching thrill.

The design, a disaster it would be
For when it rained, we swam, you see.
Snow brought us aching bones and flu,
And in August flames not a soul dared pursue.

The tree, a symbol, of love and grace
In the heart of our home, it holds its place.
A piece of heaven, it still remains
Standing tall, defying wind and rains.

T.A.

Your Eyes

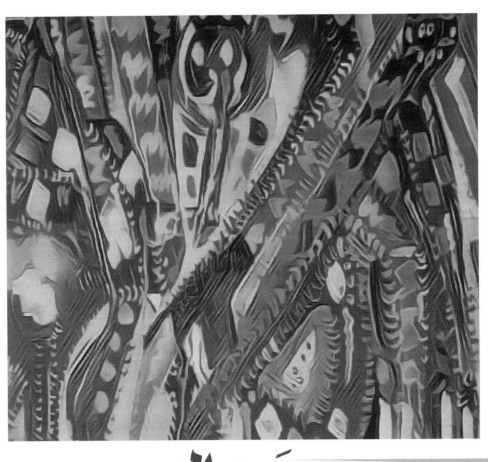

عَيناكِ

Your eyes, two diamonds in the snow,
Twin springs, a gaze that glows.
Cheeks, ripe as a Levantine apple,
Two halves, a fruit that's sweet and ample.

Breasts, two peaks, a rippling treasure
With grace and beauty beyond measure.
Knees, shins, pinkies, forearms too
Each part a twin, I'm in awe of you.

How many twins do you possess?
It seems like a never-ending quest.
From the same spring in the snow
A question, a mystery, don't you know?

Your eyes, two verses, a hidden art
Hid from prophets, a precious part.
Two blue planets, a celestial sight,
A white cloud surrounding a shining light.

Stars in space, a cosmic view,
Two lakes where sparkling stars queue.
I swim in them, I drown in bliss,
In them, I hit, in them, I miss.

"Who are you?" I asked with a sigh.
"All lovers at once, for you I die,"
She replied with a bold delight
"My twins were made for you, hold tight."

O language of forests, birds, and rain,
Your eyes, two signs of beauty, remain
Gifted from heaven, to the most beautiful queen
In them, I see, a world unseen.

H.A.

The Idiot

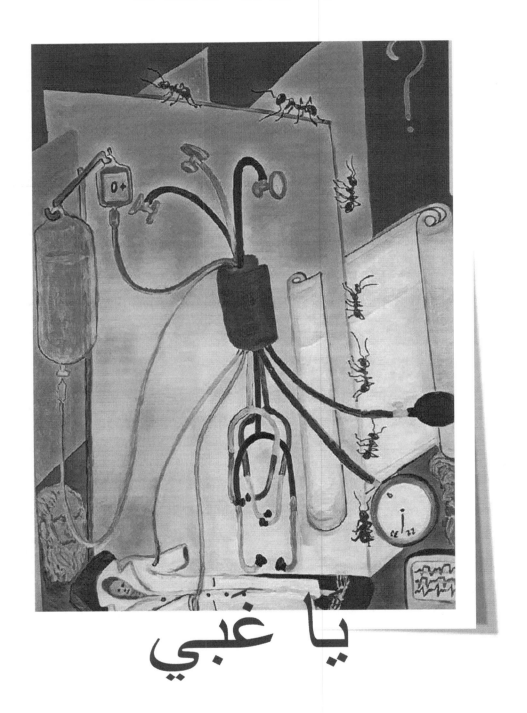

يا غبي

She spoke with soft conviction,
Her words, like gentle rain,
"Why must you be so ignorant,
And rely on machines in vain?

I am not here to be examined,
Or to have my food prescribed,
Oh Doctor, please look into my eyes,
And see the beauty that resides.

They call me Hasina, a name so fair,
A rose amongst the thorns, they say,
And all who know me, they all pray,
That the evil eye will stay away.

We've met before, in this very place,
Your heart was mine, but now it's misplaced,
On this day, your ignorance shows,
Dumber than stupid, this much one knows."

And with that rant, she turned to leave,
Her scent, the only thing to grieve,
As she vanished from my sight,
Her words, a lasting, gentle light.

H.A.

I'm not Myself

A different soul I am, so let me be,
My memories flow out like waves at sea,
My wound is deep, with poison in my vein,
So let me scatter pearls like shooting stars again.

Crazy it is, to be in such distress,
My search for love caused great duress,
A memory I wish I could live again,
Even in captivity, ignoring my pain.

H.A.

A Bewildered
Tear

هِي دمعة

حَارَت

With a heavy heart, I packed my past,
The pains and regrets I couldn't surpass.
Bidding farewell to hope and dreams,
Saying goodbye to all that it means.

It is a bewildered tear that died in my eye.
Yes, it was time for me to say goodbye
To my love and our memories untold,
Leaving behind the stories of old.

My heart pounding with the force of pain,
No rest will come, it will remain.
It almost burst out of my chest,
My blood pouring out, a final test.

I step into the silence alone,
My love says goodbye with a sigh and a moan.
Our love still virgin, pure and true,
But it's time for us to bid adieu.

She tries to hold back her tears and rain,
Her heart breaking, driving her insane.
But it's time for her to move on,
Saying goodbye, and with me be done.

H.A.

She Asked for
Her Past

طَلبَت ماضِيها

Echoing whispers in my mind,
Of love letters, pictures, and sighs.
A gift from her, once so divine,
Now lost in time before my eyes.

She asked me to forget her right away,
Forget her walk and where she was,
And erase the words we used to say,
And delete our messages, because,

Tomorrow she'll wear a wedding gown,
Accompanied by oil's elite.
Her father bought her love with a crown,
Leaving me in sorrow incomplete.

She asked me to forget her fast,
But not till the sun forgets the earth,
And trees forget their verdant past,
And ocean waves forget their birth.

How can my skin forget her touch,
Her love letters, memories, and kiss
The gifts she gave, and more so much,
That once filled all my heart with bliss.

H.A.

On Your
Wedding Day

فِي يَومِ زَفافِك

My love, my green April,
I seek to forget you, but cannot hide
From the words that haunt me. Before your leaving
Drop something of you within my crazed heart,
A kiss hidden among the roses for me to cherish.
I gaze upon my star, seeking solace
In the thoughts of the rising sun.
Tomorrow, my dear love,
The biggest wedding will take place.
My heart blesses your green dress,
Hoping to protect your name from gossip.
I promise, My Love,
I will burn our past, the smallest of love letters,
Forgetting the days we chased butterflies and brushed their
    wings.
Throwing water and roses and sugar at each other,
And the times we got drunk without wine.
But most of all, I promise
I will forget your lips,
The wine-red essence I drank from them.

H.A.

Forbidden

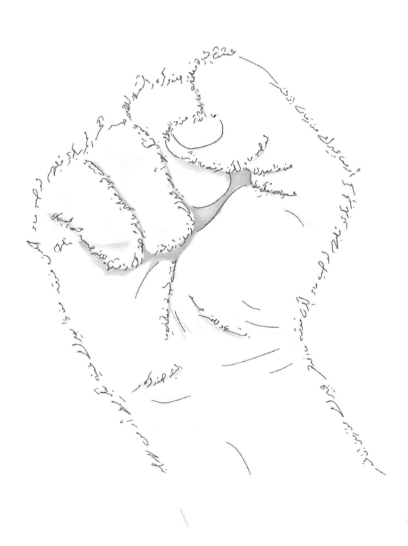

ثورَة

مَحظُورَة

Forbidden, I am a rebel, a threat in ink and rhyme.
My pain and anger, a tale of centuries untold.
Forbidden fruit, with seeds so bitter and divine,
A history of neglect and sorrow, left to grow old.

Don't delve into my pages, the secrets I hold,
The knowledge I contain, a sight to behold.
Dispose of me like trash, ignore the truth I unfold
But in your heart you know, you have a story untold.

So, bleed me not, I'm still forbidden, you see,
Who are we kidding, this truth we can't hide.
Your deity in his heaven, won't bless or set me free,
The reasons are known, your ignorance and pride.

Why, trust me, you're forgiven, for you are being thrown
Into a world that keeps you blind, that takes away your choice.
But deep down you know, you're more than just a pawn,
And in these words I speak, there's a voice that gives you voice

So, heed these words, this call, to break free from your cage.
Embrace the truth and knowledge that lies within these lines,
And rise above the shadows, to a world free from age,
Where you can make a difference, and your voice will shine.

T.A.

Abandoned
Body

الْجَسَدُ

الْمَهْجُورُ

Like ants on the hunt,
That swarm and devour their prey,
Carrying the dead.
O my deserted form,
Misfortunes crowd and converge around you,
In death I am held.
The body of a bird,
Once strong and full of life, now
Borne by tiny hands.
And so, it is with me,
Deserted and alone, yet
Still accountable.

H.A.

Sentenced to
Death

أُودِّعُها مَحكوماً
بِالإِعدَام

I saw my love, walking slow and shy,
With a book held close, her eyes met mine.
Her "hello" filled the air, with a warm embrace,
And for a moment, we lost both time and space.

Oh, sweet lipped angel, how I'll never forget,
The memories of you, I'll keep them yet.
The sun of misery sets on the landscapes of my heart,
Leaving you behind, it tears me apart.

Her hand in mine, I felt her pulse rage,
With a flick of her finger, she turned a page.
Her cheeks red, love in her eyes,
What would I say, what if I lie?

She wants love words, she asks with a gesture,
But I can only say farewell, with my heart full of pressure.
My pride stops me, from telling her why,
But the black clouds follow, and I must say goodbye.

She stood behind the door, confusion in her eyes,
How could a promised road, go unfinished and unwise.
I walked away, on this bumpy road alone,
Leaving behind, the pure water of her lips,
her waist, her braids and her throne.

H.A.

Ember Road

طَريقُ الجَمَر

A path with embers scattered wide,
I walk with care and treat my stride.
My guts, my chest, my heart of sin,
How do I treat the fire within?

I turn to Lord, give me the grace,
To handle pain with patience and pace.
And may those who threw the coals be reformed,
Their ways of hurting others transformed.

Years pass and still I feel the burn,
A dead man walking, my heart yearns
For forgotten green eyes, so kind and warm,
Illusions of love, of peace and calm.

Oh, my homeland, torn and in strife,
I hold tight to my love and life.
The sun will rise, I'll never forget,
And keep the green light shining yet.

H.A.

Euphrates

يَا فُراتِي

Along the banks of Euphrates fair,
A vessel, I made of my hands with care.
To scoop the sweetness, a river divine,
Of life and heaven, a gift that is fine.

For thirsting earth, for sowing and birds,
And all the living, your grace is heard.
In you, I wash, I swim, I play,
And let my worries slip away.

But bombs they fell, destruction they brought,
Bracelets broken; your people fought.
Buildings fell, but still you run,
To a future bright, where your work is done.

Daughters and sons return to you.
Oh, good river, Euphrates, it's true,
I will come back, to drink once more,
Of water sweet, that I adore.

H.A.

Your Wounded Cross

صَلِيبُكِ

الجَريح

There once was a man, quite forlorn,
Who felt his heart, deeply torn.
He thought of his sweetie, oh so brown,
And wondered if he'd fallen into her trap and drown.

His wounded heart begged for heaven's grace,
While papers searched for his thoughts to trace.
He hoped the pain would cease and fade,
And tears and blood would dry up, he prayed.

His distant hope was his greatest foe,
With a cross that crucified him, you know.
It stopped him from writing, even crying,
And his sweetie's hand that lay there, gently sighing.

He felt like the gods' winter cloud's great smack,
His dear one's wounded cross had pierced his back.
He longed for a word or a tender kiss,
To give his heart the greatest bliss.

H.A.

A Letter to Destiny

رسَالة إلى أقدَاري

With a brush of red tears, I write a eulogy
With my groans, I pour out all my sorrows
And I come to you, the art you've created in my heart
Is it war, or love that we wage?
Yesterday,
You left scars, took away my dreams with cruelty
Sealing eternal pain in my heart
Leaving valleys so deep,
I stumbled and fell
Now,
I'm in pursuit, running from the depths of despair
Loneliness creeps in, death chasing my every step.
I gaze at the lip of the valley, try to rise above
But I grow dizzy, the climb too much to bear
Do I give in or fight on, conquer or succumb?
It's a battle to hold on, but to let go is harder.

My values, a triad of oppression:
Silence, sadness, death, my weary back bent
At the valley's base, I paint a picture of you
And turn stones into a night watch, a life of solitude
A mystic monk and wanderer, always on the move
Digging for peace in the walls, my fate unknown
(Oh my destiny)

H.A.

The Poet's Pouch

جعبه الشاعِر

The poet, with his verse,
Invited to tour the universe's poles,
What secrets does he hold?
What's up his sleeve, they ask,
The answer:

A smart bomb's task,
Killing only children, a stark truth.
And buildings, too, destroyed,
By a missile, oh, so overjoyed,
Pregnant bellies also pierced through.
What does the poet do?

He speaks of a thief, now a minister too,
Bribery as common as the morning dew.
If he empties what's concealed,
Revealing the truth, what will be revealed?
If to the poles of the universe, truth will be unveiled.
Will the poet still have a place to dwell?
Or will the truth send him straight to hell?

H.A.

Uprooted

الْمُهَجَّر

Oh Destiny, be kind to me,
I've just learned to stand so tall and free.
My broken branches I mended with care,
Why are you skipping with your scissors to tear?

I was once rooted in soil so red,
Denied the Euphrates, taken abroad instead.
Some leaves turned dry, others withered away,
Yet my branches grew back, in a foreign land to sway.

You uproot me once more, with a promise to survive,
You say you know me; I'll flourish and thrive.
Tossed by the wind, just a branch, barely green,
I fell down, too tired to stand, or so it seemed.

But many months passed, and I understood,
That I could grow roots, fight and be good.
I dug into the earth, thick and wet,
Not too deep, for I knew, you'd uproot me yet.

I took what I needed, drops of near water,
And grew branches that learned to soar and alter.
I flap them with pride, with the strength that I hold,
So, bring forth the challenge, uproot me if you're bold!

T.A.

Lessons in Life

دُرُوسٌ فِي الحَياة

Beware of wolves that roam the night,
With sharp fangs yearning for a bite,
Their bodies strong and sleek, a fright,
A danger to the sheep in sight.

The generous ones will always share,
Their house with food and drink to spare,
A warm welcome, is always there,
A comfort to those who visit there.

But the miser's house is dark and bare,
No light, no food, no welcome air,
A cold and lonely place, beware,
A place where none should dare to repair.

A friend, in times of trouble, fair,
Will come to help, with care to spare,
And seek no fees, with love to share,
A comfort in an ordeal, they're always there.

The moons, they shine, with light so bright,
But it's their sun, that gives them might,
And birds, in flocks, they take flight,
Together, soaring, till day turns to night.

H.A.

Behind a Smile

خَلفَ كُلِّ ابتِسامَة

Behind each smile, a story untold,
Of pain and sorrow, so rarely shown,
With cheerful grins and a laugh so bold,
They hide their hearts and their truth unknown.

A casual "How are you?" with a smile,
A response of "I'm fine," so bland,
But thoughts take them to a darker aisle,
Where tears flow, and hearts pump sand.

"I'm always fine," they say, with a smile,
But their eyes, they beg for a listening ear.
So look beyond, see the pain and the trial,
And with a gentle heart, let them be clear.

So next time when you ask with care,
Look deeper, and show your kind heart.
For only then will they trust and share
Their burdens, and let you play your part.
A helping hand, a listening heart,
That's all it takes to heal their scars.

T.A.

Flame of Love

شُعلَه الحب

My love, can you see it?
The moment is almost upon us.
It's time to reveal the truth that's been burning within me,
Our love, a mere hologram, a distant memory.

The flame that once consumed us,
Has long since flickered and died.
But I held onto it for your sake,
Until you had healed from the pain inside.

I loved you truly, but it wasn't enough,
I couldn't give you what you needed,
And this burden of guilt I've carried,
Has led me down a path, unheeded.

I never intended to bring you down with me,
To drag you into the abyss of my despair.
You deserve happiness, my love, with or without me,
So, I'll set you free, to seek it out there.

The flame of our love maybe gone,
But fear not, my dear, for you now possess
The ingredients to light a greater fire,
One that will warm and protect you with finesse.

So let your soul shine bright,
And bask in the glow of love's warm light,
For you are loved, always and forever,
Even if we're not together, you'll never be alone, never.

T.A.

My One Regret

نَدّمِي الوَحِيد

They spoke of you yesterday
And I tried to play it cool
But inside my heart was aching
And tears threatened to pool

I hid my eyes, wiping my face,
Faked a smile, and took my place.
"I'm happy for you," I said with grace,
Though inside, I felt I was erased.

Joking about you, I wished you the best.
But for him, I felt nothing but unrest.
I gave you to him, his wealth and might,
I let you go, to protect you from the night.

I fought my heart, my lips, my hands,
My skin, my everything, for you; I took a stand.
Because I wanted you to thrive,
And I couldn't bear to see you suffer, or not survive.

Forgive me if that was selfish, but now you have grown
Children, happiness, and a life of your own.
Your photos, your smile, your happy weight,
Only one regret, that one moment too late

At the bottom of the stairs, you at the top,
Your hazel eyes, asking me to never stop
Kissing you, without asking to be kissed,
My one regret, that moment I've missed.

T.A.

I am My Birthplace

أنا مَوطِني

Born into pain, I tried to flee,
From the country of my birth, set my soul free.
So, I walked the Alps, let snow embrace me,
Baptized my spirit in the Danube, sipped Bordeaux wine
heavenly.
Broke Turkish bread, kissed the fiery pepper,
Tongue twisting in accents, French, English, and other.

Black feathers, I plucked them out,
Black irises, I tried to bleach,
Burned my photos of ashes and drought

Turned up the music, got lost in trance,
Danced and danced to forget the pain,
But it followed me, my every glance.

Wherever I looked, I saw myself,
Bleeding and burning,
Freezing and flooded, trying then crying.
My face, a reflection, staring back in hunger.
In white tents I was,
Floating in rivers,
Buried under rubble,
Hung on a spear, I was dying.
No matter where I ran, I couldn't escape,
For in every scene, I was there, a part of the landscape.

So, I've come to a stop,
My running away is done,
I'll face the truth, I'm Syrian,
That's where I've begun.
My black feathers I'll let them grow,
My eyes I'll let shine,
For I am the land that birthed me,
A rebel, by design.

T.A.

Thank you for purchasing this poetry book, the profits of which will all be donated to families affected by the devastating events in Syria since 2011, as well as those affected by the earthquake that hit Turkey and Syria on the 6th of February 2023. The poems you've read tell a story of survival that begins with love, and concludes with acceptance of fate rather than surrender to despair. Father wrote nineteen of the poems, I wrote nine, and we both worked on the illustrations. We aimed to mirror the journey that unites us as humans regardless of our race, colour, and origin. We all smile when we love, and we sometimes cry. We all feel loss, pride, grief and most of all, we all hope and aspire for a better future. A future that takes us back to the river that birthed us.

As Father says,

> "Daughters and sons return to you.
> Oh, good river, Euphrates, it's true,
> I will come back, to drink once more,
> Of water sweet, that I adore."

We shall return to you, oh my Euphrates.

Dr Thaier Alhusain

Follow us for more on:

Facebook: @ThaierAlhusain, @HashemHsain
Twitter: @ThaierAlhusain
Instagram: @6abibak

Printed by Amazon Italia Logistica S.r.l.
Torrazza Piemonte (TO), Italy

45121722R00038